Guru David's

Self-Esteem
For
Imperfect People

Includes!
The hidden components of Self-Esteem:
Our Self-Expectations
& Our Self-Perceptions

An original work by
David John Sheridan
aka Guru David

When you know better; you can do better!

Updated May 2021

ISBN:978-0-9932355-6-6

Published by Sheridan Publishing May 2021

DEDICATION

I dedicate this book to all the lives that have been savaged and lost as a consequences of low Self-esteem.

The wonderful lives that could have been lived; had those people had the opportunity to change their self perceptions.

Those perceptions that were tempered by chance remarks, deliberate callousness, circumstances and lifestyles.

To the wonderful gifts that the world has lost from the Arts, Sciences, Literature, Design and Innovation as a result of Others failing to see the courage that it takes to bring a new idea into the world and put it up for examination.

To the hope that people like me try to bring into the darkness of ignorance.

To better lives in the future. And to people more able to enjoy the life that they live; so that they can take their rightful places in the Legions of happy Humanity.

It is your human right to have the best life that you are prepared to have.

So take back your life from those who would misuse it and make it something that you are proud to own and call your own. *Guru David*

David John Sheridan

iv

David John Sheridan

To destroy is easy and takes little imagination.

To build that which we have the courage to imagine can take a lifetime.

To undertake a project of self-improvement and development, to better yourself and the World is a sign of someone with the courage to succeed.

Success comes from persistence, determination, dedication, being willing to accept and make mistakes, and having worthwhile goals that we can aim for and achieve.

David John Sheridan

CONTENTS

CONTENTS

ACKNOWLEDGMENTS

As I approach the threshold of a new future, a very hard and difficult period of my life is being left behind.

In amongst all the hardships, there have been wonderful lessons about the true nature of life, people and the societies that we create.

I have found myself questioning the purpose of many things; including Life itself.

In amongst all the difficulties I began to see the wonders which exist in life all the time; but that we can become immune to seeing and that gets lost behind all the noise.

All too often people look but do not see and listen but do not hear; in our lives we are experiencing a new form of blindness and deadness.

At times I thought that whatever created the Universe must have started with a sense of humour. Now I know that they did.

Life is a series of Opportunities, some of which are Golden.

I would like to acknowledge and accept the Golden Opportunities of living that the Creator of the Universe has given to me and every other person on this planet.

To help with this there is: The Way of Vartis.

Self-Esteem For Imperfect People

Finding Your Self-Esteem

Let your journey begin!

CHAPTER 1

Self -Esteem

If you are reading this book and you have bought it yourself, then you may well have read other things about Self-Esteem.

I know that over the years I have read, studied and listened to a lot of different material related to improving my life. This included: How to books, articles, audio programmes, courses, training programmes and other people; many of whom claim to be experts.

Despite my desire to fix and improve this thing that they called Self-Esteem, I found that the perceived wisdom that was being offered to me just did not do the job. What was it that I was missing?

People could tell me about Self-Esteem until they were blue in the face, they could shout at me as loud as they could, they could even try and force it into me by frightening and intimidating me; but none of it worked.

It became something within me that I could feel the affects of (emotions and feelings), experience the effects of (consequences); but I could not really get to grips with it so as to get rid of it or change it in the right way in the situations that mattered. Why?

I seemed that all the stuff that I tried to engage with just could not help me deal with this "negative lump" that existed inside of me and which was screwing up things in my life. Why?

With reflection, looking back over the many years that have passed; I can now understand what was wrong with the perceived wisdom and the "Expert knowledge" that all those other people claimed to have and traded in.

In reality they were failing to understand the real nature of the problem that they were offering me solutions too.

All these experts were great at selling but did not actually understand the reality of Self Esteem.

Bullshit is great for mushroom but not for people with low or no Self Esteem.

I realised that if you don't really understand the real nature of the problem and you suggest a solution; well the odds are that it won't really fix it. Simply because you can't!

How often do people say to us:

- Build up your self esteem.
- Develop a thicker skin.
- Don't be so sensitive.
- Don't wear your heart on your sleeve.
- Grow up.
- Don't be so stupid.
- Be stronger, more determined, more aggressive, be harder, etc.
- Be a Winner!
- Work harder!

Let me ask you:

How well has all that advice worked for you?

What I am going to do in this book is look at what I think Self-Esteem really is and not regurgitate all the bullshit that other people have been telling us for all these years.

I am going to look at how I think Self-Esteem really works.

I am going to look at how I think Self-Esteem is really constructed within each of us.

Then I want to look at how we can improve, develop and better manage our own Self-Esteem.

I will look at Self-Esteem at a level, and in a way, that you are unlikely to have done so in the past.

As you are not mushrooms; I guarantee that there will be no more bullshit!

I will include sections where you can make notes as you read and which you can refer back to later. And we will have a working section specifically for you.

So let's get started.

In normal terms this is how we understand Self-Esteem.

Self: A Persons or things own individuality, essence or substance.

Esteem: Think favourably of, regard as valuable or worthwhile.

So to have Self-Esteem we need to think favourably of; regard as valuable or worthwhile:

Our own individuality, essence or substance.

This seems so simple that we should all be able to do this; but we can't.

So what else might really be going on?

Time to kick all the bullshit we have been told to the kerb.

In my work with many people over the course of decades and from all my work with The Human Algorithm® Project; the following is clear to me.

So many people fail to understand our real problem; because Self-Esteem is actually a more complicated process and it includes many things that are hidden from us.

Self Esteem is not one thing but it is a product of many other things.

Self-Esteem is a Confluence.

Self-Esteem is a flowing or coming together of different life aspects; both past and present, and in that process it produces something as a consequence – Self-Esteem!

The Self-Esteem it produces can be very Positive, very Negative or somewhere between the two.

This Confluence doesn't only produce Self-Esteem, it also produces other things as well, including:

- Confidence
- Well-being
- Happiness
- Inner peace
- Purpose
- Our Internalised Personal Expectations
- Our Internalised Self Perceptions
- Our Acceptable Self-Identity

So we get to Self-Esteem through the Confluence that each of us has in our lives.

It turns out that finding Self Esteem is a journey to Self Esteem and we find it on the journey that we take.

Don't let this scare you or worry you.

You see you are living with this each and every day. It is part of you and you are part of it.

Think of it like streams joining together and making a river: "The River of your Life" which will always be flowing in one direction or another.

The difference with your river is that you can, by conscious choice and actions, choose the direction in which you want your River to flow; Positively or Negatively.

Don't panic at the thought of it. I am not going to offer you some quick fix and blame you if it doesn't work. We have had enough of that bullshit.

What we will do is to explore the Confluence, see how it works, understand its effects and affects; see how we can influence things in positive ways; then see what we want to do.

Remember that I said that the River of your Life always flows in one direction or another?

The Confluence has influenced the direction of your life to date.

It will continue to do so each moment of your life.

If you choose to do nothing, then the River of your Life will take whatever direction it will and this will probably not help you.

If you choose to do something, with:

"The Correct Application of Actions"

Then you should be able to change the course of the River of your Life; by influencing your Confluence.

Remember that water in a river will always take the easiest path and so will your life if you just let it flow in any direction that it chooses.

By creating dams and making channels we can change the direction of the mightiest of rivers and use the path of the water for beneficial purposes.

So it is with the River of our Lives!

What you need to realise is that by doing nothing you are making a choice. That choice will have Negative or Positive Consequences.

The choice to do nothing means that you are also choosing to give up control and are accepting that whatever happens, will happen and you will live with whatever it is.

You are handing over the control of your Life Journey to someone else who is not going to be living it and who does not have the investment that you have.

By choosing to do something Positive, with the Correct Application of Actions, you are choosing to attempt to influence the course of your life in a Positive way.

Because we are Imperfect People we are not always going to get things right. However; we can increase our chances of doing so.

We are not always going to get the result we want. However; we can increase our chances of doing so.

By continually working towards a Happier, Positive, Beneficial and Successful life; we can increase our chances of getting it.

So do you want to be a passenger in this thing or do you want to be in the driving seat?

Notes: ....
....
....
....
....
....
....
....
....
....
....
....
....
....
....
....
....
....
....
....
....
....
....
....
....
....
....
....
....
....
....
....
....
....
....
....
....

AFFECT

THE EMOTION AND/OR FEELING
WHICH WE EXPERIENCE.

EFFECT

WHAT WE DO WITH OR AS A RESULT
OF EXPERIENCING THE EMOTION
AND/OR FEELING.

CHAPTER 2

Ripples in the pond of Life

Regardless of what we do or say we cannot pause or rewind the process of life; no matter how much we might want too.

Our lives will always move in one direction: From Now; into the future.

What we can do is influence our lives: Either in a Positive way, a Negative way or in a Passive way as it moves forwards.

It can be helpful to think of our lives being divided into these three components:

1. The life which we have already lived and cannot change. This creates our history; life experiences and knowledge which we can recall and be influenced by.

2. The life which we are living here and now; today! The life that we live, in the moment in which we experience it. The real Present!

3. The life which we expect to have in the future; which has yet to happen and which can be changed: Regardless of what anyone else will tell you.

Components 2 and 3 are ones which we can still influence and change. Number 1 creates a legacy.

Every day that we live becomes a "yester-day" and

part of our past; which can influence and effect every tomorrow; and our future.

If we are not going to try and influence our lives today, then the direction of our lives will continue to be influenced by that which has already happened in the past. Logical right!

Many people say:

- That the past is a forgotten land.
- That the past is gone and forgotten.
- That the past cannot influence you today if you choose for it not to do so.
- We cannot influence events but we can influence how we react to them.

So with this simple application of such well versed knowledge why can we not simply ignore all of the bad and negative things from our past and design ourselves a perfect (or at least a better) future?

Could it be that it is simply just not that simple?

Are there more lies that we are all being told that we need to strip away before we can get to the real truth?

- Let me ask you: Have you ever dropped a stone into a still pond?

If you have, you would have watched the splash of the stone entering the water and then the ripples as they move away from the splash.

The ripples get further and further away and then gradually they disappear.

If you continue to drop stones into the same place with increasing frequency you will see that the ripples begin to develop a continual pattern on the surface of the water.

If you look; you will see that the surface of the water, some distance away from where the stone was dropped, is affected by the stone being dropped.

Now imagine that instead of one stone that you dropped two, three, four and more and more.

Eventually the surface of the water becomes a mess of splashes and ripples which collide and consolidate. Let's call this Turbulence.

Our lives can be compared to the still pond.

When we are born our lives are still and have a perfect surface.

As we develop and grow, life and circumstances begins to throw stones into our still lives and disrupts things.

Sometimes they are very small and inconsequential stones, sometimes they are very consequential stones and at other times a great big rock is thrown into our Life pond.

At times we just feel the ripples of disruption because we are unaware that someone, somewhere, has just thrown a great big rock into our life pond and it has created turbulence. We don't always see the rocks that are thrown at us.

At other times life and circumstances can be throwing rocks into the Life pond of someone you care about, know or are going to know in the future.

It is in this way that ripples in the pond of Life of one person can move from one pond to another and travel further afield.

Now we all know, that in the real world, when we stop throwing rocks into a pond that the surface of the pond returns to its previous state.

So let's think of our Life pond a little differently.

Imagine that our ripples not only affect the surface of the Life pond but also the overall shape.

You see in real life if we throw stones into a pond, they displace water and the displacement minutely affects the architecture of the pond as a whole.

With a single stone we don't really notice it. But keep adding the stones and, over time, noticeable changes occur.

The water level rises and touches new things as it rises. The shape of the floor of the pond changes as the stones sit beneath the surface of the water.

So a single stone not only causes a ripple, it changes the ground on which it lays and it changes the overall shape of the pond.

As it is with a real pond, so can it be with our Life ponds.

We may see and experience the buffeting of the water as we are hit by the ripples. Then as the ripples pass by we can think that things have returned to normal.

However there is still the question of "the affect" the object that caused the ripples is having underneath the surface.

Then there is the question of how the object has caused the overall shape of your Life pond to change.

Often when the ripples have passed we can forget that something still lies beneath the surface and that we can continue to bump into it and be affected by it.

So how does this affect us and our Self Esteem?

When the Turbulence of Life goes on for long enough we begin to think of it and accept it as being normal.

When the Turbulence is missing, we unconsciously are continuously preparing to deal with its effects and affects. This is a normal human reaction.

Some call it: Waiting for the other boot to drop.

Depending upon the type of Turbulence we are having to experience, our minds and bodies will behave in different ways.

As a consequence of our minds and bodies behaving in different ways; so we will also act and respond in different ways.

All of us, as we go through life will experience what I call "The Legacy Affect".

That is that certain parts of our history and our life experiences and knowledge will continue to be part of our lives and influence us either directly or indirectly in an ongoing way.

We may be consciously aware of this or we may not be consciously aware of this. It is however possible to understand that these things do exist and then begin to work with those Legacy issues.

I am not saying that all or our problems are caused by issues or events from our past.

What I am saying is that there may be things which have occurred before today which are causing ripples in your Life Pond.

They may be small things or big things or things which appeared to be inconsequential at the time.

With many of these things it is the way that we have interacted and continue to interact with them that can continue to cause Negative or Positive Turbulence in our Lives and the Lives of others.

Often with these things there are simple, apparently

innocuous steps which we can take, which can lead to managing these Legacy Affects in different ways; which in turn can lead to them ceasing to be a problem or as much of a problem for us.

There are a number of ways of working with difficult and obscure Legacy issues but they are outside of the scope of this book, so I will not go into them here.

Guru David provides help in this area with The Way of Vartis and The Human Algorithm® Project.

Contact him if you would like his help.

david@gurudavid.co.uk

Notes: ....
....
....
....
....
....
....
....
....
....
....
....
....
....
....
....
....
....
....
....
....
....
....
....
....
....
....
....
....
....
....
....
....
....

Chapter 3

Unintended Consequences

Have you heard about "so and so"?

Just look at the way that she looks today, pity that she got dressed in the dark!

With a backside like that you would think that they would have more sense that to wear...

Yes that colour suits her; pity that its last seasons...

Yes of course she is my wife's friend, but when you look at her; you could just...

I just can't tell them the truth about their behaviour and what I really thought of...

If they ever say anything like that to me again I am going to wait until they are asleep and...

Well yes, but if they had actually done it right in the first place...

How often do we overhear conversations or hear comments that may be about us or related to us one way or another?

How often do we use our imagination to fill out the details that we have failed to correctly overhear or that we have failed to correctly see?

How often do we take the statement made, the

angry outburst, the personal attack, the physical attack, the verbal aside; and put our own spin on it?

How often:

- Do we add our own fear?
- Do we add our own anxiety?
- Do we add our own desires?
- Does it confirm what we really think?
- Does it confirm what we really feel?
- Does it make us continue being a certain way?
- Are we afraid that we have been found out?

There can be enormous "Unintended Consequences" from events that are the result of us putting out fears and insecurities together with something someone said or did.

These ripples in our life ponds can last for many years and even for a lifetime.

I know that I personally have experienced Unintended Consequences that have influenced my own behaviour, my view of myself in the world, my relationships with other people and many other things.

- If it really doesn't matter to you at any level; then it will not touch you or affect you. No one is immune to this; so stop your bullshit.

For Unintended Consequences to occur there has to be feelings and emotions that are able to attach themselves in some form to the "Event" from which the Unintended Consequence happen.

What creates the Unintended Consequence is the Combination of the Feeling (and/or Emotion) that is brought to the surface by the event or caused by the event; and the Affect or Effect that the combination of them produces at the time; which is remembered and henceforth: Is Acted Upon.

It creates what we call: A Human Algorithm that you will experience and then use; repeatedly.

Whether this is caused by:

- Embarrassment.
- Fear.
- Unhappiness.
- Feeling uncomfortable.
- Feeling Inappropriate.

As well as experiencing Negative consequences there can also be Positive Unintended Consequences. Such as:

- Feeling proud.
- Feeling valued.
- Feeling wanted.
- Feeling desired.
- Feeling a part of something.
- Changing your view or perception.

The experience that the Unintended Consequence produces within us may be Positive or Negative in its nature; but we will have noted it in some way and it will have "Stuck with us" or "Clung on to our Lives".

Some of these "Unintended Consequence

experiences" are naturally absorbed into our lives and cease to have ongoing Effects or Affects; they are transitory.

Others are not absorbed and can be an ongoing influence which we may or may not continue to be aware of; these are ripples.

Unintended Consequences can occur from Positive events, Negative events and apparently innocuous events. This is why they are called "Unintended".

In order for the Unintended Consequences to attach to our lives; all we need to have is a fragile emotion, an exposed fear, a worry in the back of our minds or an insecurity.

In other words: We just need to be:

"Imperfect People"

As human beings we have many different aspects of life to which it is possible to attach what we have witnessed or experienced; that somehow connected with us.

- Once it becomes attached we then have something that can drop into our Life pond and cause ripples.

One characteristic of these Unintended Consequences is that they can repeat endlessly and permeate the fabrics of our lives.

They can revisit us within our awareness and

outside of our awareness.

- It is when these things become part of the fabric of our lives and fall outside of our conscious thoughts that they can become most damaging because we cease to notice them but still experience them.

They can feed our fears, confirm our worst suspicions, provide the evidence we need to justify behaviour and a whole host of other things.

What is annoying about these Unintended Consequences is that you never know what is going to stick and what isn't.

The Unintended Consequence of your life will be part of the Confluence of your life.

- The Confluence is that place where the strands of your life come together and where the product of that coming together is created.

    The Confluence has many components which produces and Affects the Self-Esteem that we experience and feel.

    Your Confluence can be influenced and changed in a planned way and it does not need to be left to fate.

What are the Unintended Consequences that you have or may have experienced in the past?

What are the Unintended Consequences that you

think you may still experience now?

Notes: ....
....
....
....
....
....
....
....
....
....
....
....
....
....
....
....
....
....
....
....
....
....
....
....
....
....
....
....
....
....
....
....
....

CHAPTER 4

Intended Consequences

In the previous chapter I focused on Unintended Consequences. In this chapter I want to consider Intended Consequences.

These are actions, behaviours, circumstances and personal interactions which are intended to be hurtful, harmful and damaging.

We can also consider those which were intended to be Positive but which ended up becoming Negative.

- The reality is; that good things happen to bad people and bad things happen to good people.

Life can be very unfair at times. People should not have bad things happen to them; but they do happen.

Regardless of where we are at in our lives; children, young adults, mature adults and those in latter life; we can still all be hurt by things.

- An adult can be as sensitive as a child.
- A big burly man can be as sensitive as an adolescent teenage girl just beginning to notice her body.
- A retired person can be disappointed in love just as easily as a teenager with their first crush.

- An overheard remark can cause crushing hurt to anyone who is vulnerable at the time.

We can never be totally immune to the consequences of the behaviours of others or ourselves.

However; we can learn to understand these things for what they are and begin to address them in Positive ways.

Some of this may be easy to do and some of it may be difficult.

All of us will find that, regardless of what we do, something will find its way into our Inner World and cause us problems: Whether this is Intended or not.

If we are unaware of what it is and how it really affects us, then we are not going to be in control of it or be able to deal with it.

- Even the people who choose to hide themselves away from life do not escape these things.

  Indeed; It may have been these things which influenced them to behave in this way. And without realising it, they are paying a very high price.

As people we have different capabilities for Self Awareness.

Some of us may be aware that something is going on inside but be unclear about what it is and how to clarify it.

Others may find that they have little or no capacity for Self Awareness and Introspection. But they have the capacity to understand that something, that they can't put their finger on, has influenced their behaviour; and this itself can present a route to understanding.

Then there are others who can only see and experience the results of the behaviour that they find difficult or unwanted.

Whatever the individual circumstances are, at some stage there is something that leads someone to the Realisation that they have something which is causing or influencing them to do things that they don't really want to do or would prefer not to do.

Many people will have the Moment of Realisation that there is a Driver or Influencer which is out of their direct control; which is causing them a problem or difficulty that they would rather not have.

Other people will experience consequences and be able to relate the undesirable experiences directly to an event. Even so, they will be unable to effectively deal with it, even though they are armed with such an apparent level of knowledge and insight.

Why?

Because all is not as it seems and there are things which we do not know, comprehend or accept.

And all of these things feed into the Confluence. That place where everything comes together to create who and what you are.

Notes: ....
....
....
....
....
....
....
....
....
....
....
....
....
....
....
....
....
....
....
....
....
....
....
....
....
....
....
....
....
....
....
....

Chapter 5

The role of Self-Expectations And Self-Perceptions in Self-Esteem

I have spent many years listening to others talk, advise, coach and mentor about Self-Esteem, Being Positive and Being Successful.

I have heard people being told:

- Build up your Self-Esteem.
- Do positive things.
- Think positive.
- Behave like you have good self-esteem and it will develop from there.
- Increase your personal confidence.... Etc.
- Behave like a winner and become one.

Sometimes this works for people, often temporarily, but what about all the other times that it doesn't work?

What is going on there?

What about all those times that we think we have solved the problem of our Self-Esteem and then we slip back to where we were before or even further?

What is going on there?

Life is a little more complicated at times; so I am going to take you to another level with this to help you to better understand this process, so as to help yourself with it.

My view is that the Relationship between Self-Esteem and other factors needs to be better understood.

If we understand this relationship better, then we can deal with it better and achieve better results.

- Life isn't a menu from which we can select certain dishes that we like.

- Life is the kitchen in which the food that we enjoy is created.

And it is the same with Self-Esteem. We have to get the right recipe and have the right ingredients to get the delicious dish of Self-Esteem tasting "just right".

So let's have a look at what I think may be the missing ingredients from so many Life recipes.

- In my view Self-Esteem is not a stand-alone item; its a stand with item.

I have mentioned the Confluence; the point at which the different strands of our lives come together, blend together and create that which we are, that which we experience and that which we do.

The Confluence also blends together that which we will become.

This creates the Opportunity for us to Influence the Confluence and as a result: Future Outcomes.

I think that Self-Esteem is part of a structure which includes our Personal (Self) Expectations and our Personal (Self) Perceptions. Putting them into a list would look like this.

- Self-Esteem
- Self-Expectations
- Self-Perceptions

They can be thought of as three legs of a table.

If one or more of the legs is short then the table is off balance and unstable. If one or more of the legs is too long then the table is off balance and unstable.

So let's take a brief look at the two legs of Self-Expectations and Self-Perceptions which help to support Self-Esteem.

Self-Expectations

Our Self-Expectations are the "real" expectations that we have of ourselves.

These are the ones that we "keep to ourselves" and tend not to share with others; as it can expose us more than we are comfortable to do so.

These are the Protected Self-Expectations that are at the Core of Our Being.

Our Core will contain the Self-Expectations which we really believe we can achieve or which we doubt that we have the ability, opportunity or time to achieve.

These are part of what we could call:

Our Personal Truths.

Our Personal Truths includes the areas in which we experience our own "Deservedness" to have and obtain the things which we want or don't want to happen.

If we really believe that we "Deserve" it then we can move Positively towards achieving it.

If we really "Don't believe that we Deserve it" then we can move Negatively and always manage to miss that which we desire at another level.

In different situations our Self-Expectations will vary.

In some situations there are no doubts or reservations; so we have no impact from Negative Self-Expectations.

In other situations the doubt is present. And through this doubt we can be subtlety influenced or we can move towards strong emotions and feelings such as naked fear.

Because of the Confluence; the coming together of these three components will allow each of these components to share part of what they are with other components.

- For example: You can't stand in a crowd of people without being affected by the mood and movement of the rest of the people.

You will, in some way, be touched by their presence.

As people we have a Common Range of Emotions, Feelings, Actions, Re-Actions and Dynamics which we create.

And as a result of what we create; we will have Tendencies towards certain Behaviours, Feelings and Emotions.

So it would be logical for our Self-Expectations to share components with our Self-Esteem and with our Self-Perceptions.

And one of those shared components is our Worthiness. How Worthy we really think we are to have what we really want?

Notes: ....
....
....
....
....
....
....
....
....
....
....
....
....
....
....
....
....
....
....
....
....
....
....
....
....
....
....
....
....
....
....
....
....
....
....
....

Self-Perceptions

Our Self-Perception is how we really "Perceive Ourselves in the World" - Our Position in the hierarchy of Life in different situations.

It's like seeing ourselves in a picture of our lives and thinking whether the picture is right or wrong.

The types of questions that we may ask ourselves at the conscious level are:

- Do I belong here?
- Is this really me?
- Do I really deserve this?
- Am I worthy of this?
- Should I really have this?
- Am I going to get found out and have it taken away?
- People like me don't do things like this?

And when we are experiencing times of difficulty:

Are we Perceiving Ourselves "Well" within our Minds Eye View or are we Perceiving ourselves "Poorly"?

One of these has a Positive and Constructive view of Ourselves and the other has a Negative and Detrimental view of Ourselves.

I bet you can tell which is which?

Balancing the Components

So how well does our Self-Esteem stand up, if our Self-Expectations and/or our Self-Perceptions are out of balance with it?

Think about this for a moment.

Our Self-Esteem generally changes in different situations. So does our Self-Expectations and our Self-Perceptions.

> We notice the difference in our Self-Esteem in specific situations where we have problems with it.
>
> And these tend to be situations which we can identify.

In other situations we do not have a problem with our Self-Esteem and the issue of our Self-Esteem does not arise.

Why?

Could it be that, in the situations where you are comfortable with your Self-Esteem; that your Self-Esteem, Self-Expectations and Self-Perceptions; all align in a Complimentary Way?

> When the Confluence of these three components is arranged in a Complimentary way; it produces Positive Results and Desirable Outcomes.

If the Confluence of these three components is arranged in a Non-Complimentary way; then we would expect to achieve something other than the Positive Results and Desirable Outcomes that we would hope for.

Therefore; It begins to become easier to understand; but it is not easy to address.

So how would we go about successfully addressing it?

Real Self-Esteem isn't really about what the World thinks of us; it is about what we really think and feel about ourselves; in the different situations in which we find ourselves.

> The Worlds perception of us can influence us by confirming or challenging what we think of ourselves.

> So if we are uncertain or confused and the World is telling us something which we doubt or cannot accept; then further uncertainty and confusion can easily be created.

> And the person can become Befuddled in the process of trying to understand and work it out.

We are unlikely to overcome poor Self-Expectations or poor Self-Perceptions by trying to force our Self-Esteem or any other single component to compensate.

If we try to push one or two of the legs of the table to be bigger and stronger to support the others; we still end up with an unbalanced table.

The simple and easiest thing to do long term is to fix the problem in the right way.

This is the real challenge and this is why so many of us have failed to respond to all the advice that we are given.

> We are trying to fix the problem in the wrong way!

It is Normal to have variations in Confidence and Self-Esteem as we move through life and experience the daily challenges that we may face.

Our challenge in life is to live the best life that we can and in doing this we can lose our way.

> *To the outside world we may appear to be successful; but within ourselves we can still feel like the failure that deep down we may feel that we are.*

The self esteem that often matters to us most is not the positive self esteem that we no longer have to think about, but the negative self esteem that we experience and which can bring down our lives.

The answers are within yourself and the ability to improve and resolve the problems are also within yourself.

The role of people like me is to help you find and access these things in a positive and productive way.

And to do that it can be helpful to begin thinking of Self-Esteem not as one single thing but as a collection of different things. A collection of different experiences and outcomes.

Really it can be helpful to think in terms of "Self-Esteems" because this is really what Self-Esteem really is:

> A collection of Positive Experiences which together produce something greater than the whole.

And it is the same with Negative Self-Esteem. A collection of Negative Experiences which together produce something greater than the whole.

Therefore; the challenge that we all face is that of putting together our own Personal Collection of:

- Positive Experiences
- Positive Actions
- Positive Attitudes
- Knowledge and Understanding
- Personal management skills
- Positive Affirmations

Which together helps produce the Self-Esteems which we want and to keep us on the right path.

I think that by thinking in terms of "Self-Esteems" that it makes the problem easier to manage and improve.

When we begin thinking of Self-Esteem as a single thing which is either Right or Wrong we create too much of a mountain to climb. And it's the wrong mountain!

By breaking it down into individual episodes of Self-Esteem it becomes manageable.

For example:

In a certain situation I have low Self-Esteem.

Now I can begin looking at that situation and see how I can manage that situation in a different way so that it impacts my Self-Esteem in a different way.

When I enter another situation where I experience low Self-Esteem I can do the same thing.

What we are doing by this process is Being Pro-Active and seeking to influence our own Confluence in these different situations.

I am trying to help you see and understand that we can all Improve, Develop and Manage different aspects of life in more positive and productive ways.

Achieving this is about small steps which when added together create a journey of Self-Improvement and Development which produces

Positive Results and a more Positive, Beneficial and Successful Life.

In all of our lives there are times when we need to make large changes and we need to deal with these times when they happen.

Sometimes we have no control over when this happens and at other times we are in control of when this happens.

The mistake people often make is that they try to make the big changes at times when they are least ready to make them.

I.e. They have not prepared sufficiently so as to increase their chances of success.

Too often in these cases "Wishful thinking" without sufficient preparation takes over from practical reality.

Like many things in life:

- An Excess in one area will not automatically compensate for a Deficiency in another.

Achieving the right balance can be an uncomfortable process to go through; but done correctly it can produce outstanding results.

Notes: ....

....

....

....

....

....

....

....

....

....

....

....

....

....

....

....

....

....

....

....

....

....

....

....

....

....

....

....

....

....

....

....

....

....

....

Chapter 6

Take a Deep Breath!

In reality there are few lives that are incapable of being improved in this world.

And if you have just said to yourself that you are amongst the few: Well you are so wrong!

The choices that we have to make with life are:

- Are we going to take part?

- Are we going to do the best that we can?

- Are we willing to experience the bad as well as the good; but not be defined by either?

- Are we willing to accept that regardless of how old, how able, how well educated, how rich or how difficult life is: That we can live a good and productive life if we are willing to do so?

- When we get knocked down; are we willing to get up again?

If you have read this far then I would say that you have what it takes to makes a difference to your life.

In my experience changing your life and being successful isn't about the big things, it is about the small steps that we take each day.

Each small step forms part of the Life Journey that we are all on.

It is also easier to take a small step and to make a small change than it is to take a giant leap or make a huge change.

In a sense the Elegant Simplicity of this is very easy to miss.

- We achieve large changes through the preparation and undertaking of small changes.

- We undertake a long journey through taking small steps each day.

- We live our lives one day at a time and we gradually work our way through decades of time.

Many people strive to implement and achieve big life changes without the necessary preparation and understanding.

This often leads to failure and Unexpected Consequences.

It's not that this approach doesn't work; it's that this approach, done the wrong way, usually fails.

A little success that you can build on is much better than a mountain of failure that you need to dig yourself out off.

GREAT LIVES AND GREAT SUCCESS
ARE THE PRODUCT OF DIFFERENT
COMPONENTS WHICH COME TOGETHER
TO CREATE THE WHOLE.

EACH PERSON ON THIS PLANET IS PART
OF THE WHOLE OF HUMANITY.

DON'T BE AFRAID TO LIVE YOUR LIFE
BECAUSE THIS IS YOUR GIFT
THAT WAS GIVEN TO YOU PERSONALLY!

SO TAKE A DEEP BREATH
AND GET INTO THE GAME
IN THE RIGHT WAY!

Notes: ....
....
....
....
....
....
....
....
....
....
....
....
....
....
....
....
....
....
....
....
....
....
....
....
....
....
....
....
....
....
....
....
....
....
....
....

Chapter 7

The Human Dynamics Matrix©
And Your Self-Esteem

I would like to introduce you to The Human Dynamics Matrix©.

I developed the Human Dynamics Matrix© to help me work with and understand different types of problems that involve people.

I also wanted a productive way of working with the people involved with the problem, so that they could achieve a better understanding of the nature of the problem and achieve insights that would be beneficial.

I thought that if I could achieve the right level of understanding of the true nature of a problem; that I could then begin to understand the true nature of the solution that the problem required.

Once you have both of these things then you can achieve the right Direction and Purpose; which the person experiencing the problem usually lacks.

Once you have these then you can begin to work out the Path that can lead you to the Successful Result that you want to achieve.

Once you have all this you can then begin to document the process so that you can confirm it works. And then collate information about successful solutions and better ways of managing and improving different types of problems.

In reality; this is an immensely complex area and I struggled for a long time trying to invent and develop a simple way of being able to work with problems that can be complex, disparate, lacking in insight, random, contradictory, etc.

However; through years of perseverance I have achieved a result that I am happy with and which I and other people will be able to use in the future and build upon.

The Human Dynamics Matrix© works with the following components both individually and collectively:

Emotions/Feelings + Psychology + Actions/Re-Actions (Behaviour) + Dynamics + Other factors

These components cover all the different forms of activities which involve people. Whether this is personal, professional or business related. Whether this is a single person, a group or a social network.

The idea behind the Human Dynamics Matrix© is that it helps to create a Map, a structure of all the different components of a problem and how all those different components fit together and produce the outcome that they do.

Think of it as mapping the Confluence so that you can understand how the Confluence works in individual cases and for individual problems.

One of the unique characteristics of the Human

Dynamics Matrix© is that it allows us to work with Tendencies that exist within each of the components shown above.

The Tendencies helps us to understand the long term implications of the position within the matrix of components; such as Self-Esteem.

Many of the actions that we take as people and many of our behaviours have Tendencies attached to them. So this is quite an important area to understand.

We can also break components down into activities in which Negative or Positive outcomes occur, so that we can get behind the obvious and begin to develop beneficial Insights into what is going on and how to facilitate improvement to or resolution of the problem being experienced.

Another thing that the Human Dynamics Matrix© allows us to do is to understand the different Ranges within which activities; such as Self-Esteem occur and the implications of where and how those various activities are taking place.

I will be explaining more about the Human Dynamics Matrix© in another book which will be titled: An Introduction to the Human Dynamics Matrix©.

To work with the different components of the Confluence requires a certain amount of knowledge and it has taken me over 20-years of hard and difficult work to achieve this.

So what we will do now is see if we can get behind your problem of Self-Esteem.

To do this we will use the workbook process so that you can write down your understandings, either within the book or on something else, so that we can work with them.

Notes: ....
....
....
....
....
....
....
....
....
....
....
....
....
....
....
....
....
....
....
....
....
....
....
....
....
....
....

Chapter 8

Analysing the Problem

The process of analysing the problem is used to help us better understand the problem and also to see if we can achieve Insights, Understandings, Awareness's and a better overall feel for what we are dealing with.

All too often people begin with what seems like the obvious problem but in reality what they are focusing on is a Symptom of the problem and confusing this with the problem itself.

What I want you to begin to understand is the difference between the Symptom that the Problem creates; and the Problem which is producing the Symptom.

A good example of this is someone with a long term problem with their weight due to their eating and Lifestyle Habits.

Usually the person wants to deal with the problem of Being Overweight and they want to do this through dieting.

On the face of it this seems like a sensible approach with an obvious Cause (bad diet) and Effect (being overweight) that can be addressed.

However this does not address the Lifestyle Habits and issues which contributed to the development of the eating and weight related problems AND which contributes to the ongoing development of the weight problem and associated issues.

I have often heard people say: "I will deal with all these other problems once I have dealt with the weight problem".

As a result the person usually goes on another diet; which almost certainly fails and they never get to the point where they feel "Good enough about themselves" to deal with the other problems.

As a result:

The cycle continues and the progression to further health problems and Lifestyle problems continues.

To deal with this type of weight problem requires the Symptoms and the Problems to be addressed in a co-ordinated way over a period of time.

> Simply put: A good diet cannot improve a bad Lifestyle (its focus is too narrow).

> However: A good Lifestyle Management programme can improve a bad diet because it deals with both Cause and Effect/Affect.

So we are not looking for the attractive quick fix which usually fails to deliver on its initial promises.

What we are after is the Robust Longer Term Solution which leads to a better quality of life.

> *The consequences of focusing on the quick fix is that if we only address the Symptoms*

without addressing the Causes; then the Causes can continue to create Symptoms which will cause you ongoing problems.

As it is with weight problems, so it is with Self-Esteem and other issues.

What I also want to make clear here is that we are not looking to make judgements, to point fingers, to say that someone could have done something better, to make someone feel useless or any other Negative outcome.

- We are looking for Education about what we want and need to do.

Education means looking at the good and the bad; the Positive and the Negative and learning the lessons that we need to from both.

We will look at the three legs of Self-Esteem and see how they fit together for the problems you experience and want to improve.

Remember what the 3 legs are:

- Self-Esteems
- Self-Perceptions
- Self-Expectations

The first step is to identify the situation or situations in which you feel that you have low or no Self-Esteem or where Self-Esteem is a problem for you.

Please be as clear as you can be with your answers as we will be referring back to these as we go through this book.

Please write down your answers to the following questions.

No.1 The Situations in which Self-Esteem **is** a problem for me are:

....
....
....
....
....
....
....
....
....
....
....
....
....
....
....
....
....
....
....
....
....
....
....
....
....
....
....
....
....

No. 2 Looking at those situations; **how** did you know that you had or have low Self-Esteem while you were involved in those situations; or on reflection afterwards?

....
....
....
....
....
....
....
....
....
....
....
....
....
....
....
....
....
....
....
....
....
....
....
....
....
....
....
....
....
....
....
....
....
....

No.3 What was it that **confirmed**, to you, that you had or have low Self-Esteem in those situations? *It will probably be an Emotion, Feeling or Behaviour; or all three.*

....
....
....
....
....
....
....
....
....
....
....
....
....
....
....
....
....
....
....
....
....
....
....
....
....
....
....
....
....
....
....
....

Now go back to the situations that you first wrote down in question. No.1

Considering your answer to that question again, take a look at your Self-Perceptions this time rather than your Self-Esteem.

No.4 How were **you** Perceiving **yourself** in **your mind's eye** while **you** were in that situation? *What pictures were in your mind?*

....
....
....
....
....
....
....
....
....
....
....
....
....
....
....
....
....
....
....
....
....
....
....
....
....
....
....

No.5 Now look at your answer to question No.1 again. How did **your** Self-Perceptions influenced these situations? Did you feel Worthy, etc?

....
....
....
....
....
....
....
....
....
....
....
....
....
....
....
....
....
....
....
....
....
....
....
....
....
....
....
....
....
....
....

Once again; go back to the situations that you first wrote down. No.1

> **No.6** Considering your answer to question No.1 again. Now take a look at **your** Self-Expectations **in** that situation?
>
> Did you really get the outcome that you really thought you would; the outcome that you Expected?

....
....
....
....
....
....
....
....
....
....
....
....
....
....
....
....
....
....
....
....
....
....
....
....
....
....

What we will do now is to look at the situations that you have written down in question No.1

And I want you to choose one or two of them, and I want you to write what you have chosen on the following page.

If you have written down lots of them in questions No.1, then just focus on one or two; the one or two which are clearest to you and most important to you.

You can always do this exercise again and take the different situations one at a time from question No.1 or write down new answers.

If you do repeat this exercise again, some of your answers may be the same and some may be different. In reality there is no right or wrong answer.

Remember that this is a process of searching for Education about what we do.

So write down the one situation that is most important to you from question No.1

....
....
....
....
....
....
....
....
....
....
....
....
....
....
....

We are going to considering the 3 legs of:

- Self-Esteems
- Self-Perceptions
- Self-Expectations

What we are going to do is to put a value to each one of these so that we can understand them better.

You may need to take some time to think about this and you may need to come back to it a few times.

This is not a contest and there are no right or wrong answers. Just put down what you think or feel is correct. You can always change it later if you want to.

Let's take Self-Esteem first.

1. On a scale of 1 to 10. With 1 being: I have no Self-Esteem and 10 being: My Self-Esteem could not get any higher. Score your Self-Esteem in that situation?

1.2.3.4.5.6.7.8.9.10

Now let's do the same with your Self-Perceptions.

2. On a scale of 1 to 10. With 1 being: I have no Self-Perceptions and 10 being: My Self-Perceptions could not be any more positive. Score your Self-Perceptions?

1.2.3.4.5.6.7.8.9.10

Now we will do the same for the last one: Self-Expectations.

3. On a scale of 1 to 10. With 1 being: I have no Self-Expectations and 10 being: My Self-Expectations could not get any higher. Score your Self-Expectations?

1.2.3.4.5.6.7.8.9.10

Now let's see what the scale tells us.

4. Where did you score your Self-Esteem?

#No. ....

5. Where did you score your Self-Perceptions?

#No. ....

6. Where did you score your Self-Expectations?

#No. ....

Looking at the numbers you have written down to questions 1, 2 and 3; we are going to get an idea of scale.

Looking at all 3 numbers that you have written down; are your numbers the same or is there a big variation?

If you have scored 9 or 10 on this for all three legs then you should not need to be concerned with your Self-Esteem in the situations that you have considered because your Self-Esteem should be high. If you are concerned by this: Why?

If you have scored about midway (5'ish) then there are things that can be done which can help you get that score higher.

If you have scored below midway then what I would like you to do is to go through the exercise again just to confirm the results that you have. There is nothing wrong with the answers that you have; I just want to make sure that we are starting in the right place.

Remember this is not about the numbers it is about what the numbers really mean to you and are they truly reflecting where you are at.

Notes: ....
....
....
....
....
....
....
....
....
....
....
....
....
....
....
....
....
....
....
....
....
....
....
....
....
....
....
....
....
....
....
....

Chapter 9

Achieving Direction And Purpose!

If I was working with someone and we were using the Human Dynamics Matrix©, we would look to understand the true nature of the problem that the person was experiencing. Then we would look to understand the true nature of the solution that their problem required.

Once we had this we would then work out Direction and Purpose: I.e. What we were going to do and why, when and where we were going to do it.

As I am unable to use the Human Dynamics Matrix© with the readers of this book we will use another method.

Our objectives will be the same: Achieving Direction and Purpose.

To achieve a Direction we need to know where we are and where we want to get too. So we will use one of your earlier answers to do this.

Let's take the answer to the question about your Self-Esteem that you wrote down on page 61.

Please write this same answer down on the following page.

The Situation in which Self-Esteem is a problem for me is:

....
....
....
....
....
....
....
....
....
....
....
....
....

My score for answer #No.4 (Self-Esteem) was:

A. #No.....................

My score for answer #No.5 (Self-Perceptions) was:

B. #No........................

My score answer #No.6 (Self-Expectations) was:

C. #No....................

So this should provide the starting point. And we have 3 digits that we can use With a maximum score of 30 across the 3 digits.

A + B + C

If we take the information above and then we asked this question:

- If we took this problem and made changes to improve it: What would these changes look like?

....
....
....
....
....
....
....
....
....
....
....
....
....
....
....
....
....
....
....
....
....
....
....
....
....
....
....
....
....
....

If we achieved this improvement:

How would your score for Self-Esteem and the others change; if this was to happen?

Would they move from what they are above at A + B + C?

And if so, to what: What would be the new numbers?

Self-Esteem would become:

#No.........................

Self-Perception would become:

#No.........................

Self-Expectations would become:

#No.........................

If the level of improvement isn't enough for you then take another look at how the problem needs to be improved or changed.

A word of caution!

We are looking for something realistic that we can work with here. You may need to break the improvement into smaller pieces rather than think of huge leaps.

Keep the final goal in mind but realise that
it may take a few steps to get there.

CHAPTER 10

The Correct Application of Actions

One of the things that I have learned is that problems and solutions have structures that can be understood and worked with.

I have worked with many people; helping them to deal with problems and to have a better life; by dealing with whatever is getting in the way of that happening.

There are certain dynamics (processes and structures) that occur again and again when dealing with people.

One of those dynamics is that people who are experiencing a problem do not really want to look at and understand the real problem that they are involved with.

They prefer to think that the problem is not as bad as it looks or that it is at a different stage of rectification than it is. In effect they Under Estimate the problem.

Another thing that they do is that they Over Estimate the ability of the solution that they are going to apply to the problem.

In effect the solution that they want to apply does not have the correct structure or ability to deal with the problem to which it is being applied.

And the third component that occurs is that the

person, business or organisation that is going to apply the solution to the problem; is not actually going to:

Apply the Correct Application of Actions.

The Correct Application of Actions includes the timing of the actions.

Many people are given solutions to problems that work if they are applied at that time and in the correct way.

What often happens is that they delay apply the solution and the structure of the problem changes.

Once the structure of the problem changes it often becomes worse and then they try to apply the solution that they previously had.

At this stage there is often a "Misfit" and the person who has delayed the application of the solution has in effect: Sabotaged the solution.

What you need to realise is that if you have just one of these components wrong, then the likelihood of success diminishes.

If you have all three of these components wrong then you will require a miracle for things to work out successfully.

And this is what so many people end up hoping for:

A Miracle!

They don't actually realise that they can usually improve or resolve problems themselves, if they begin to do so the right way; rather than the wrong way.

The Correct Application of Actions is actually a very powerful statement.

Think of what this is saying to you?

There is a way to do this thing that makes it work better; are you prepared to do it?

If you apply the Wrong Application of Actions; are you prepared to then correct it and do it the Correct way for the Problem and the Solution that the problem requires?

You see what this is; is Different Thinking!

The Correct Application of Actions moves through both the Problem and the Solution that the problem requires.

It is about choosing to Manage that which goes into the Confluence and that which comes out of the Confluence; so that you get a result which you prefer to live with.

Through the pages of this book I can try and help you to understand the powerful implications of this process.

The Correct Application of Actions
has an Elegant Simplicity about it.

Most of us have experiences of something working well and producing a positive outcome that we liked.

> In effect; for that to have happened, all the Components would have fitted together just right and we experienced the delicious result of Success.

Solving any problem, achieving any goal, changing any outcome; is all about bringing the Right Components together and Achieving the Right Blend.

> If you can't be bothered to bring the Right Components together, if you can't be bothered to Achieve the Right Blend; then you require more and more luck to get a successful outcome and luck is seldom around when you need it.

If you Apply the Correct Application of Actions then you diminish your need of luck and begin to take control over the things which matter to you.

Just doing something, isn't Applying the Correct Application of Actions. It is just doing something.

So the next thing which we are interested in is:

Go back to:

What the Improved Problem would look like on page 67.

Then have a think about:

What do you think the Correct Application of Actions would be in order for that problem to Improve in the way that you describe?

Write your answer below.

Then write those actions down here.

....
....
....
....
....
....
....
....
....
....
....
....
....
....
....
....
....
....
....
....
....
....
....
....
....
....
....
....
....
....
....
....
....
....

So now we have:

1. An understanding of the situation that you have a problem with.

2. An understanding of how the components of Self-Esteem, Self-Perception and Self-Expectations play a part in that situation.

3. A scale for each of these components.

4. A clear idea of what the Improved situation would look like to you.

5. An idea of how this Improved situation would change the scales for your Self-Esteem, Self-Perceptions and Self-Expectations.

6. An understanding about the Correct Application of Actions and how failing to do this reduces your chances of Success.

7. My permission to be an Imperfect Person; so that if you make a mistake, then you can try and get it right the next time and so on.

And if we put all this together we have **the outline for a Plan** that you can begin to work with and use.

In the next sections I am going to look at different things related to the components of Self-Esteems, Self-Perceptions and Self-Expectations.

I will look at both Negative and Positive things which I think will be helpful and useful for you.

Notes: ....
....
....
....
....
....
....
....
....
....
....
....
....
....
....
....
....
....
....
....
....
....
....
....
....
....
....
....
....
....
....
....
....
....
....
....

To deal with Fear, Uncertainty, Doubts and other things which cast Shadows over our Lives; We simply need to shine a light of Education, Understanding and Knowledge on to it.

Then we can pause, take our time to get our bearings and begin to do the things we need to do.

CHAPTER 11

Building Negative Self-Esteems

I am going to talk about a few of the different aspects that end up with us Building Negative Self-Esteems.

Not because this is what we want to do but because if we understand how we do it; we can avoid doing it and control it better.

You may recognise the different aspects that I will look at.

Building Negative Self-Esteems is a process that happens quite naturally for human beings. We can do it without noticing the effort and resources that we have to use to develop and support an ongoing Negative process.

- Everyone builds Negative Self-Esteems at some point in their lives.

Earlier I mentioned the Life Pond and the stones that get dropped into the water. I mentioned that even the smallest stone can cause a ripple and have an overall effect upon the shape of the pond.

Building Negative Self-Esteems is about collecting stones that have been thrown into your Life Pond or in the general area of your Life Pond and using them to build little islands in the water.

And every now and again we pick up the stones from these little islands and throw them into the water ourselves. And obviously this causes ripples that affect us and our Life Pond.

And every now and again we will find that we have created a dam in our Life Ponds and we will bump and crash into it.

How we navigate our lives can be determined by the stones, the islands, the ripples and the dams that we participate in creating.

About now you might be thinking:

"So it's all my fault!"

No I am not saying that at all. What I am saying is that you have more control over this process than you ever realised or accepted.

Let me explain.

You would think that with so many people having lived in the past and with so many people alive today that we would have this emotional and feeling stuff all sorted out.

It seems that as the older generation dies off all of these wonderful life experiences, skills, understandings, insights and knowledge are lost to the rest of us.

What a tragedy of life.

The reality seems to be, for most people, that each generation has to work out the life processes which involve growing up, growing older, having relationships, having children and all the other things that life holds.

Schooling may give us a general education but when it comes to life skills, life knowledge and life experiences; we seem to have to get these the hard way.

As we become older we acquire Life Skills, Knowledge of Life and Experiences of Life. This is regardless of what type of life you live, where or how.

This process creates a Random Education Process that requires someone having the luck to be born into the right circumstances and social network.

If they have good luck their circumstances help to equip them with additional Positive life skills and experiences which they will find useful.

If they are less fortunate then their circumstances will not provide them with the positive life experiences, in fact they may well have to deal with negative life experiences from a very early age.

Life is a funny thing and it has an ironic sense of humour at times.

People born into good circumstances end up just as screwed up as people born into less fortunate circumstances.

No-one is immune to creating Negative Self-Esteems when the circumstances of their life are aligned that way.

In reality whatever circumstances we are born into; by the act of simply being born; we will bring something unique into those circumstances that has the ability to change them.

As a baby you have no influences other than Being.

You cannot contribute anything other than by Being a Catalyst for events that are not controlled by you.

Over time your natural dispositions will begin to emerge and then you will become part of the Confluence of Life.

The introduction of you into the circumstances that surround you, means that you are part of the Confluence that exists for those circumstances.

This means that you can and will effect change at some point in time.

In reality our ability to effect change is often dependent upon other people and the circumstances in which we find ourselves.

At times the only way that we can change the circumstances in which we find ourselves is to leave them. Either permanently, periodically or on a temporary basis.

Eventually, in life, we all have to arrive at the point where we have to accept that life is; as it is and deal with it from there.

If we want it to be different; then we need to do something that can assist in making it different.

If we just sit around waiting for things to improve; well they may just get worse.

I am a believer in that simple phrase:

- Evil flourishes when good men do nothing.

At times we just have to stand up for what we believe in, for what we want, for what we believe to be right, or to stand up against that which we believe to be unjust, wrong, inappropriate, unfair or not something we wish to be a part off.

This is one of life's challenges:

Standing up for yourself and taking for yourself the life that is yours to have. If you are prepared to do, what you need to do, to get it.

Each of us is born with this Right!

We don't need to be smart to understand feeling good or feeling bad.

We don't have to be able speak so as to tell others how we feel. Because we are able to show others how we feel through our behaviours.

Often what we are not told, simply because it is difficult for so many people to personally understand and convey to others, is this:

OUTWARDLY OUR BODIES NATURALLY AGE AND MATURE.

INTERNALLY

WE DON'T NATURALLY AGE AND MATURE.

SO WE CAN HAVE AN OLDER BODY WITH THE INTERNAL MATURITY OF A TEENAGER.

Notes: ....
....
....
....
....
....
....
....
....
....
....
....
....
....
....
....
....
....
....
....
....
....

Chapter 12

Stopping Putting Yourself Down!

Have you got into the habit of Putting Yourself Down?

This habit is really easy to slip into.

It happens when someone has been exposed to a lot of Negative Feedback, Negative Focused People; or when someone finds themselves having to deal with and put up with Negative Situations, which they are told they can't change.

If you have been exposed to these things then you probably have the Negative Habit to some degree.

Even if we have not been exposed to lots of Negative Feedback from others or exposed to Negative Focused People we can still develop this habit.

There is another process that I have seen, which helps someone develop the Negative habit of putting themselves down and that process is this:

Someone lives a life or they have lived a life where there is an Absence, a Void of things which should be there but are not there; or are not there in sufficient quantity at the right times.

That Absence or Void is a lack of things like the following.

An Absence or Void of:

- Positive feedback.
- Positive affirmations.
- Recognition of Positive experiences.
- Validation of our efforts.
- Time for yourself and doing the things which you really like and enjoy doing.
- Things which add up to Valuing yourself as a human being and a valuable member of society.

You see a Void can become as solid as any wall and just as impenetrable.

The Void becomes a desert, a wilderness, a lost land.

As such; it becomes somewhere where we do not venture. Somewhere where we are afraid to go.

To avoid going there we develop habits, ways of dealing with the risk.

You see:

- Putting yourself down.
- Giving yourself no value.
- Undermining what you do.
- Not valuing what you do.
- Giving yourself a beating before others can do it for you.
- Always putting yourself last.

These are all parts of a process that has good intentions at its centre but which gets Corrupted.

The simple process of:

Protecting and Not Exposing ourselves.

There is a point at which Self-Protection or the protection of others through Self-Sacrifice; turns into something which hurts you rather than helps you.

It is an easy thing to fall into.

How do you recognise if you are putting yourself down?

If I was to say:

- The little voice in your head.

 Would you understand what I mean?

If I was to say:

- That negative thought that jumps into your mind when you thought that you had done something well.

 Would you understand what I mean?

Have you ever watched people having a conversation where one person keeps pausing as they speak, because they expect the other person that they are talking too, to interrupt or say something: but they never do?

As a result the person speaking gets more and more confident and eventually they stop waiting for the other person to speak.

And the person who keeps pausing finds it more and more difficult to say something as they become more nervous and timid about interrupting the other person while they speak.

In effect this is what we can be doing in our own minds and in our own lives.

When we do something we pause, we wait:

> Allowing the space to exist for the Negative Comments that we know are coming.

If they are delayed we can find that we wait for them: Expectantly!

Waiting for "It" can even get uncomfortable and cause us stress.

Then eventually "It" comes and we can breathe a sigh of relief as normality is restored.

"It" confirms what we suspected all along!

We are rubbish at doing whatever it is that we suspected we were rubbish at doing.

And "It" goes on, "It" becomes established in one area of life and then progresses into other areas of life.

The wet blanket of uncertainty, fear and doubt spreads.

Changing this process is simple but not easy.

It takes practice. And because we are Imperfect People, we won't always get it right.

Sometimes we may shout for the wrong team. The competition; the Negatives.

But that is OK!

You see we have a get out of jail free card:

> We are Imperfect People and we are allowed to get things wrong while we work to get them better and to keep them better.

What if we have a really bad day or a really bad week?

That's OK because we are Imperfect People and we are allowed to do so. Because tomorrow I can be better, I can do better and I can feel better.

So what do we need to do to change and improve things?

Well what do we do when we are having a conversation with someone and we want to change the subject?

- Sometime we wait for a break in the conversation.

- Other times we make little signals that indicate that we want to make a point.

The trouble with this is that we can miss the opportunity to speak and be heard.

We can get railroaded by the other Negative voices and not be heard.

Why should they stop speaking to us and telling us what they think of us; because we have not done anything to interrupt the conversation in a way that makes a difference – Yet!

Well just like when you are having a conversation and you want to talk about something else:

- You can change the subject of the conversation in your own head and have your say.

- You can let the other voices speak and begin speaking yourself and choose to listen to what you are saying.

So Change the Conversation that you are having with Yourself!

How would you do this in the real world?

You would assert yourself and make sure that you got your point across – that you were heard.

This is the same. Make You hear Yourself.

When you do something well; give yourself a pat on the back and say: Well done me!

If you do something not so well; give yourself a little praise and say: Well I did that as well as I could this time and next time I am going to do it better.

Before you start something; give yourself some praise about the attitude that you are going to bring to the task and then give it your best.

Begin to do jobs very well. Even the smallest and simplest of jobs can be done in a way which you can look at it and say; yes I did that, isn't it good!

You may be about to wash the kitchen floor, cook a meal, go shopping, drive to work. All of these things can be done well and give you a positive boost.

With the things that you don't do so well. Just say to yourself that you are going to try just that little bit harder to get it done better and to do it without putting yourself down.

All of these simple things begin to build up into a chorus of Positive Messages that you are feeding into your Self-Esteem.

Another thing to do is to begin using Positive Affirmations and Positive Quotes. You can find one on this website: www.vartis.co.uk

All of these things feed into your Confluence.

Gradually they begin to change the shape of your Life Pond. The Negative stones reduce and Positive stones take their place and Positive Ripples gradually begin to spread.

Just take it one day at a time.

Notes: ....
....
....
....
....
....
....
....
....
....
....
....
....
....
....
....
....
....
....
....
....
....
....
....
....
....
....
....
....
....
....

Chapter 13

Stopping The Enemy Within!

One of the most powerful Allies that we have can also be one of the most powerful Enemies that we have.

I am talking about the Long Term Internalised Negative Processes that we all have and are influenced by.

Let's call it "The Enemy Within".

- What does this do?
- How do we recognise it?
- How do we deal with it?
- How do we get it on our side?

I like to think of The Enemy Within as a "Frustrated Force".

You see within each of us we have the desire and motivation to do things. If this energy does not have a clear direction to work in; then it will find its own path.

Our own fears, worries and anxieties are perfect places for our Frustrated Force to go to and to attach too.

And once our fears, worries and anxieties connect with our Frustrated Force; well it just connects with it and achieves a purpose.

The purpose is to develop and maintain the thing

that it has connected with and attached too.

So you see our Internal Frustrated Force wants things to do. It wants to survive and grow!

Just like water, our Internal Frustrated Force always takes the path that is available to it. In the absence of you providing it with one it will find its own; whether its Positive or Negative.

Having some fears, worries and anxieties is a healthy thing. Having too many or over blown ones becomes a problem.

So we need a balance where we have some which surface appropriately and some which occur when we are feeling sensitive about something which matters to us. We may call this Appropriate Concern rather than Manic Behaviour.

All of us at some time or other are going to have a moment where fear becomes strong and it can be debilitating. We have to examine it to see whether it is rational and appropriate when this occurs.

If it is not rational and appropriate then it may be that Internal Frustrated Force latching on to something.

About now someone reading this may be saying to themselves that they are too busy, too tired or too rushed off their feet to have any Frustrated Force left at the end of the day.

Being over tired, exhausted and stressed can be a perfect hunting ground for that Frustrated Force.

You see when you are too tired, exhausted and stressed, you are frustrating all those other aspects of life that you are missing out on.

Those holidays you haven't had, the new car you would really like, someone else to clean the house, someone else to get the shopping, no time for your partner, no sex life, and the list could go on and on.

This is the Void.
The Absence of that which you need or want!

So in reality there is no such thing as I don't have the time or the energy for this, because it is your capacity for wanting and needing things which you do not have or cannot get which helps to create the Frustrated Force.

Have you ever wondered why being Negative is easier than being Positive?

Because it is easier!

You don't have to do too much because everything you need to be Negative is within you and easily found about you.

Next time you are near a very negative person or group of people being negative about something, take your time and really look at what they are doing and really listen to what they are saying.

Often they have become trapped in a cycle of behaviours which they are unhappy with but feel unable to do anything about.

That Frustrated Force needs to go somewhere!

How do we recognise our Frustrated Forces at work?

- How often have you done something which you are not happy with having done?

- How often have you joined in conversations which are Negative in their nature?

- How often do you fall into behaviour and actions which you don't really want to do but you end up doing them anyway?

These are all examples where our Frustrated Forces can be at work.

How do we deal with it?

Well your actions are telling you something.

You have Energy that wants to be put to work doing something. If you can't find anything Positive for it to do; then it will find its own Purpose and take the easiest path it can find.

It really is a case of putting a little more effort into understanding what you are actually doing and why.

If you have had a conversation a hundred times already this week; well why are you going to have it a hundred and one times?

Is this time really going to make it or you feel better?

Instead: Look around for something nice to talk about instead or to involve yourself with.

If you are about to do something which you don't like and don't like yourself for afterwards; well why not take a few moments and think of what else you could do with the time that is more Positive and Productive.

Sometimes the thing to do it to pause and actually take some time for yourself.

What you are looking for are Opportunities to turn that Internal Frustrated Force into a Beneficial thought, action or deed.

Now don't go over the top with this and remember that no-one is perfect. Allow yourself to be Imperfect at times and challenge yourself to be better at times.

How do we get our Frustrated Force to be our Friend?

In reality we may need to break some habits.

Some of these habits are ones that we may have

had for a very long time.

Now breaking habits means that you have to do something different. Doing something different often feels uncomfortable. This will often make people frustrated which feeds into the Frustrated Force.

The reason for this is that your body and mind is attempting to maintain what you are used to doing. And you are trying to do something else; that it is not used to doing.

You are trying to guide that Frustrated Force in another direction and apply it to another purpose.

Depending upon the habits you have and the circumstances around it; habits can often be changed in about 30 days. This time frame is dependent upon the type of activity and the frequency of it.

Now what you can't do successfully is this:

You cannot try to change the direction of your Frustrated Force to try and trick yourself that your life is better than it is.

For example:

That bad or difficult relationship cannot be improved by you telling yourself to be more tolerant and that you should not mind being beaten up or abused.

You might get away with it for a little time but the reality is that you will know what is really going on.

Another reality is that at times we have to make tough choices and tough decisions.

If we don't make them; who will?

Life gives us challenges and we have to deal with those challenges in the best way that we can.

We are not always going to get things right, or be perfect; because we are all Imperfect People.

And do you know what: That's OK.

When you are fighting yourself;
you cannot win and if you do win; you lose!

Notes: ....
....
....
....
....
....
....
....
....
....
....
....
....
....
....
....
....
....
....
....
....
....
....
....
....
....
....
....
....
....
....
....
....
....
....
....
....

Chapter 14

Creating & Building
Positive Self-Esteem

All of the Human Dynamics have a structure and Self-Esteem is part of Human Dynamics.

As we have gone through this book we have looked at and examined that structure.

I have introduced you to the Confluence and I have asked you to think about Self-Esteem in conjunction with Self-Perceptions and Self-Expectations.

I have introduced you to concepts such as the Internal Frustrated Force.

Part of what I have been trying to do, is to Educate you. To show you that you do not have to be a Passive Instrument and that you can be a Pro-Active Individual who can begin to Take Control of certain aspects of your life in a different way than you have before.

I am offering you a choice of Paths to take.

Keep on the Path that you are on and see where it takes you. Or change Paths if you are not happy with the one that you are on.

Changing Path doesn't have to mean massive life changes.

Think of it as moving more towards the Sunshine rather than the Shadows.

Do you want to have more Sunshine in your life or do you prefer more Shadows?

It's your Life and so you can make the Choice.

So how do we create and build Positive Self-Esteem?

Creating and Building Positive Self-Esteem is something that can be done.

People do it all the time, often without any awareness that they are doing so.

We begin by using the tools that each of us has.

We are not all aware that we have these tools and we are not all aware that we have been given Permission to use them at the moment of our birth.

I don't know what your life is like and I don't know about the constraints and difficulties that you have had or that you experience today or that you will face in the future.

What I do know without any doubt is:

You have control over your Internal World. Your Internal World is your Dominion; the space that is exclusive to you and that no-one else can live within – they simply physically cannot live there; you can.

That Internal World is your Life Pond. People can throw stones, cause ripples, build islands and create dams BUT you have Dominion!

At any time, in any situation, at any part of a process YOU can begin to change things.

I am not saying that it will be an easy or simple thing to do. It may not be.

But what you have to realise and accept is that if you want to change something, then you are not happy with it. If you are not happy with it and it can be changed; then why put all that effort into maintaining something that you are not happy with?

A good place to begin to create, develop and maintain Positive Self-Esteems is to follow the process that I outline in this book

This will help you to focus more clearly on what you want to achieve and why.

At this point there is another concept that I want to introduce you to.

- The Incompressible Period of Time

The reason why so many quick fixes fail is because of the Incompressible Period of Time.

Put simply; certain things have a process that has components which requires certain things to happen in certain ways over certain periods of time.

For example: If you were to cut your finger and it bled you would clean the cut and put a dressing over the wound.

To speed up the healing process you may put antiseptic on the wound and keep the dressing clean. Over time the wound heals and things are fine.

Now let's assume that we want the wound to heal faster, much faster.

So we know that keeping the wound clean helps and that changing the dressing helps.

Therefore; if we clean it a lot more often and we constantly change the dressing then it will heal faster – Right!

Of course not.

In fact the opposite is likely to happen. Over cleaning keeps the wound open and it is then more likely to become infected. Changing the dressing too often begins to interfere with the natural healing process.

So the correct healing of the wound is subject to the Incompressible Period of Time that is required for the body to naturally heal itself.

You will also face the Incompressible Period of Time in different aspects of life.

If you try to overcome it by applying lots of effort you may well pay a price for doing so.

It is usually better to understand the Incompressible Period of Time and work with it.

Developing Positive Self-Esteems is something that has Incompressible Periods of Time attached to it.

When you are working with different aspect of your Self-Esteem allow reasonable periods of time.

Remember the 3 legs of the table:

1. Self-Esteems
2. Self-Perceptions
3. Self-Expectations

All of these feed into the Confluence.

If things get out of balance begin to work on getting them back into balance.

To create; we dream, we imagine, we innovate and we develop.

We are prepared to make mistakes and move beyond them and try again until we get the results we want.

Notes: ....

....

....

....

....

....

....

....

....

....

....

....

....

....

....

....

....

....

....

....

....

....

....

....

....

....

....

....

....

....

....

....

....

....

....

....

....

....

Chapter 15

Doing Positive Things
And Having Achievable Goals

Life has a funny way of happening around us. And then one day we wake up and see that Time has passed as well as Opportunities.

We have probably all heard sayings like:

Life is too short to...

To understand the reality of this we often need to have lived a certain amount of life and have a certain amount of Life Experiences to look back on.

In life, it is better to look back at Positive Experiences rather than Negative Experiences.

In truth; life is going to be made up of both types of Experiences.

We can adjust our lives so that when we look back over them we have more significant Positive Experiences to look back on than Negative ones.

There are stages in each of our lives where we will look back over our own histories and we will have Regrets. The Regrets we will have will tend to be about the things which we wanted to do but never did.

We will tend to have fewer Regrets about the things which we did do and wish that we hadn't.

And in a sense this provides a Formula For Life.

- Live a Life doing Positive Things, in Positive Ways to achieve Positive results.
- Do what you can to Live life today; rather than keep putting it off until tomorrow.
- We know that Today exist and we hope that tomorrow does.

We achieve a better quality of life by taking the time to think about our lives and then taking action to achieve the outcomes which we want.

To achieve we need to Plan. Our Life Plans do not need to be lengthy documents with massive amounts of detail.

Our Life Plans should contain an outline of what we want to Do and Experience.

As you move through your life other things will be added to and taken away from your Life Plan. This is normal because our Priorities change as we go through life.

Life is always a Recipe to which we can add ingredients or take them away. We are looking for the right flavours, taste and textures to give us that Positive Living Experience.

Don't be afraid of life because at the end of your Life Journey you will realise that the fear was another ones of life's little jokes: You never really needed to be afraid at all!

Live Well!

To fear that which is real;
is sensible.

To fear that which is unreal;
is a folly.

Chapter 16

Positive Lifestyle Management

I began developing Positive Lifestyle Management Solutions in 1997-8.

For most of my life I have been interested in problems and what causes the problems. I have also been interested in solutions and what makes the difference between solutions that work and solutions that don't work.

As I grew up I began noticing patterns in things and wondered why other people ignored things like this.

I was always interested in improving my life and the lives of the people that I cared about.

I was prepared to work hard and to work long hours to achieve this. I always tried to bring other people with me to improve their lives.

I left school at 14 years of age. I was bright but there were a lot of things going on at the time that were not conducive to being at school.

My life has not been an easy one. There have been lots of different challenges and obstacles to deal with and overcome.

When I left school another level of my education began in the University of Life. This can be a tough place.

I went to night school, went on courses, read

books, listened to my Uncles, Aunties and Grandparents when I went to stay with them in Ireland. And I generally tried to make sense of all this stuff that they call life.

I went into business for myself and tried a variety of different things as I tried to improve my life and develop a better quality of life.

I guess that I have a Curiosity of Life that has been battered at times but somehow manages to brush itself down, find new strength and continue.

I personally tried many of the personal improvement and business development solutions aimed at dealing with problems and improving things.

I looked at and tried the "Quick fixes" and the "Get Rich Quick" solutions that are marketed to all of us who want to fix a problem in life.

I read lots of books, listened to lots of audio programmes and attended courses and workshops.

I paid for some pretty expensive training and I even took a year out and went to College full time for a year doing a specialist course.

In life there is always someone who makes achieving the things we want seem simple.

With any form of problem there always seems to be people who are saying that they have the solution to problem (X).

I always found that when it came down to it; the easy thing to do is talk and the difficult thing to do is to actually make it work.

That's what I was always interested in and wanted to know:

How do you actually make it work?

The number of times that I felt like a freak or an idiot because I just could not get the results that these experts said that I should or could get.

Gradually over the years I began to look at these things in another way.

I began looking at the true nature of the problems and the true nature of the solutions that the problems required.

I also began looking at what you really needed to do, **and be able to do,** to match the problem and the solution; so that you could achieve the result that you wanted.

I found that so many solutions sound or seem to be attractive because they offer a simple and easy solution.

However the real success rate for an average person using these solutions would be low.

I was interested in solutions that could be applied to problems where the success rate would be high; and if it wasn't we could identify why that was not the case and fix the problem.

This required Different Thinking!

I began to trust my own judgement rather than the judgement of those promoting solutions and telling me that they were experts.

When I began dissecting their offerings I kept seeing things that were being ignored; and that other things that they were saying were just plain wrong.

I was also surprised that so many people who were marketing, selling and providing solutions did not actually understand the structure of the solution that they were providing or the structure of the problems that they were claiming they could fix.

In reality they were just sales people.

To begin seeing these things requires that you have taken the time and put in the effort to see that things are not as they seem.

You don't need to become an expert but you do need to apply common sense.

In reality the consumer has as much responsibility for how these things have developed, as the sales person selling them.

The consumer wants an easy quick fix which is as painless and rewarding as possible.

Sooner or later it stands to reason that someone will try to give you what you want.

My approach has always been to try and do the job right. To do what really needs doing.

This means not ignoring the things which are inconvenient, difficult, hard to address or difficult to comprehend.

These are often the things which, if they are brought into things, makes the difference between success and failure.

I also look at problems and solutions as being a part of our Life Journey.

I view them as part of our life and something about which we can make choices; do we continue to experience them or would we like to change and replace them with other experiences.

I also consider timelines differently.

- In reality if someone wants to be successful they want to be successful for the rest of their life.
- If someone wants to deal with a problem then they want to deal with it for the rest of their life.
- If someone wants to be happier then they want to be happier for the rest of their life.

- If someone wants to be fitter and slimmer then they want to be fitter and slimmer for the rest of their life.

A person or business may want a problem solved quickly. Just because you want it solved quickly doesn't mean that it can be solved quickly.

Often the reality is that you can begin to develop and apply the solution to the problem quickly; but achieving the desired outcome is a longer process.

When I have worked with people, there are what I would call "Challenging Points" in the process.

These are times when someone begins to feel better about the problem that they have had. They may even feel elated.

Because they feel better about the problem they begin to re-evaluate how they saw the problem when they sought help for it.

This often leads them to conclusions like:

- It's not as bad as I thought it was.
- I could really have dealt with this by myself.
- I feel better now and I don't really need your help any more.

What they don't realise is that this is all part of the Dynamics of the problem.

In resolving problems there are often High Points

where the person with the problem feels great and that they can cope on their own. In reality this is usually very fragile and they don't realise it.

Another thing that usually happens when you resolve problems is that we encounter Low Points.

Times when the problem bites back and all the pressures return, along with the very strong Tendencies to return to your previous behaviour.

To deal with these types of Problem Solving Dynamics I began viewing problem solving as a Lifestyle Management, Improvement and Development process.

Whether I am working with an individual or a business I take the approach of Lifestyle Management, Improvement and Development.

The reality of how I see things is that a business is really not much different from a person.

- A person has a life, a business has a life.
- A person has finances, a business has finances.
- A person has health issues, a business has health issues.
- A person has Well-being issues, a business has Well-being issues.
- A person has problems, a business has problems.
- A person has relationship problems, a business has relationship problems.
- Both of them have people in common.

I also think that if we look at problems as being part of the normal life cycle then we are not such a freak for having a problem that we cannot sort out. Its normal.

I think that we can resolve and improve problems in a better way, by making solving and improving problems a part of our Lifestyle Management processes.

Remember that you are:

An Imperfect Person.
And that's OK!

Notes: ....
....
....
....
....
....
....
....
....
....
....
....
....
....
....
....
....
....
....
....
....
....

Chapter 17

Beware The Slings And Arrows

It tends to be consistent. It happens just when you think that everyone is with you. It catches you by surprise. What am I talking about?

The Slings and Arrows of life.

William Shakespeare mentions the Slings and arrows of outrageous fortune in a play called Hamlet. *The passage is repeated at the end for you.*

I don't want you to become a scholar of Shakespeare and I am certainly not. However; this soliloquy simply demonstrates the questions of life that we all have and which any right thinking person has.

Hamlet was written sometime around 1599-1602 AD.

Hamlet shows that over 400 years ago people were struggling to come to terms with life and how to manage the different aspects of it.

If we go back to each Civilisation that has ever existed we find that life has these patterns of existence and living which repeat again and again.

My interpretation of the Slings and Arrows is this:

Should I put up with what life throws at me; or should I stand up for myself; for the things that I want; for the things which I hold to be right and true?

In other words: Should I rock the boat and risk losing all that I have?

Where I am going with this is:

> That having self-doubts, anxieties and feelings of inadequacies is normal for people. It has been for many hundreds and thousands of years. So why should now be any different?

All of this relates to the questions that people have about Self-Esteem and other aspects of human life.

> The Answers to the Questions that we hope will lead us to understanding life and having a better life.

The reality is that Life can be and is; tough at times.

Some people are lucky and they have few major problems as they go through life. Others find that their lives are challenging from the time that they are born, until the time that they die.

It is easy to become jealous of those we see whom appear to have better lives than the ones that we live.

However jealousy tends to spawn resentment, destruction and negative behaviour which can envelop the person who is jealous.

In reality; very few lives are deprived of happiness, contentment, laughter, smiles and fun. Our challenge as human beings is to make the most of them when we experience them.

Even in times of war, famine and other natural disasters people get to the stage where they stop crying and begin to do something about the problem.

Living any form of life is about Being and Doing.

This is regardless of whether you are living a Positive Life or a Negative Life; you will still be, Being and Doing.

There are many people who have privilege lives in all cultures and at all social and economic levels.

Many of these people are not what might be considered "Deserving" of the lives that they have.

However this is just one of the peculiarities of life and it will not change; because it is part of human nature.

Why not take another view of all this?

> Why not "Be Deserving of the Life" that you have by making the most of it. And by using every opportunity that comes your way and that you can make?

If you sit back and wait for great things to happen,

then you have embarked on a fool's errant of enormous proportions.

Life is about Opportunity.

The opportunities that come and go and the ones that we can influence, create and partake off.

The finest and best opportunity that a person can have on this planet is that they were born. For without this nothing else matters.

Build on this golden opportunity to take part in life and make the most of every day.

> If we can have a single genuine smile in a day, then that day has been worthwhile.

Many a Dictator has found that the Human Spirit eventually finds its way out of the pit of despair that they create; and into freedom.

It is a pity that those of us who live in free societies allow ourselves to become Shadows of the people that we have the ability and opportunity to be.

Stop being a Shadow and become a real person.

Live in the Sunshine of life!

This is a reproduction of a soliloquy from Shakespeare's great tragedy – Hamlet.

Hamlet's "To be or not to be".

I have put it into sections which I think makes it easier to read and understand. This does contain language from the time.

The opening question introduces the fundamental uncertainty that characterises the passage as a whole. If you don't get it; don't worry about it.

Notes: ....

....

....

....

....

....

....

....

....

....

....

....

....

....

....

....

....

....

....

....

....

....

David John Sheridan aka Guru David

To be, or not to be: that is the question.
Whether 'tis nobler in the mind to suffer
The slings and arrows of outrageous fortune,
Or to take arms against a sea of troubles,
And by opposing end them?

To die: to sleep;
No more; and by a sleep to say we end.

The heart-ache and the thousand natural shocks
That flesh is heir to, 'tis a consummation
Devoutly to be wish'd.

To die, to sleep;
To sleep: perchance to dream: ay, there's the rub;
For in that sleep of death what dreams may come
When we have shuffled off this mortal coil,
Must give us pause:

there's the respect
That makes calamity of so long life;
For who would bear the whips and scorns of time,
The oppressor's wrong, the proud man's
contumely, The pangs of despised love, the law's
delay, The insolence of office and the spurns
That patient merit of the unworthy takes,
When he himself might his quietus make
With a bare bodkin?

Who would fardels bear,
To grunt and sweat under a weary life,
But that the dread of something after death,
The undiscover'd country from whose bourn
No traveller returns, puzzles the will
And makes us rather bear those ills we have
Than fly to others that we know not of?

CHAPTER 18

Moving On and Letting Go!

In life we all have things that happen which we want and things which happen that we don't want.

At times we have to accept something that has happened, or is happening, and we need to move forward with it. If we don't we can become stuck.

> Life can be painful and heart wrenching at times.

> Losing something or someone who was very precious to us can decimate our lives at that time.

> We can even have trouble letting go of positive events that we continue to try and rekindle as the flame of memory dies down.

The reality is that we cannot hold on to everything from our past because we then don't have room for new experiences.

It does not matter how old or how young you are or what stage of life you are in; or whether you are in good health of bad. Life still has things to offer which are of value.

By letting go of something and allowing it to take its proper place in our history, we are not abandoning the people and the precious memories which they may have shared with us.

We honour people more by allowing them to take their rightful places in our lives and by giving them the credit for the things that they have done.

Sometimes we also have to give them the responsibility for the things which they did which were not so nice.

As people we have the ability and the freedom to make choices. It may not always be clear to us that we have.

Sometimes we have to pay a price for what has happened and for what is happening. It can be unfair, unjust and just plain wrong. But we are the ones that get stuck with the bill.

Pay the bill and move on. Because by now you will probably have paid the bill many times over and haven't realised that you don't have to keep doing so.

Many of the things which happen to people leave wounds and scars.

At times we have open wounds which do not heal and which other people may keep open.

Sometimes the only remedy from a hurt is the distance we can put between ourselves and those who cause the pain. Sometimes it works and sometimes it doesn't.

Regardless of whichever country you are in,

regardless of whatever religion you follow, regardless of your gender, regardless of your age, health, education, wealth or any other aspect of humanity:

Life can only be Improved and made Better by those who are Living it, Doing it and Experiencing it.

Not by those who are hiding from it!

Notes: ....
....
....
....
....
....
....
....
....
....
....
....
....
....
....
....
....
....
....
....
....
....

Chapter 19

You Are The Most Important Person In Your Life!

I can try and help you with all the skills and abilities that I have. However: The single most important thing you need to come to terms with is this:

<u>YOU</u> are <u>THE</u> MOST IMPORTANT PERSON
<u>in Your Life!</u>

This is not about arrogance, or about being self-centred, or about being big headed or about having an over inflated opinion about yourself.

This is a truth that it took me a long time to accept and to understand.

I hope that it won't take you as long as it did me.

So let's look at what this really means.

From my point of view I am speaking about people who are trying to have good lives – even if they don't have them yet.

Those seeking to do positive things like holding down a job, running a business, having a family, being a good member of their community, helping others when they can, etc.

These would be people that I would say are trying to live life in the Sunshine.

On the other hand we have those who spend their days caught up in a world of drugs, alcohol, crime, abuse and other activities which cause harm to themselves and to others.

These are people that I would say are living their lives in the Shadows.

Personally I think that a lot of the people who end up living in the Shadows, have or will have the opportunity to begin living in the Sunshine some time in their future.

Some will take advantage of that opportunity and some will not.

Whatever the situation, good or bad, you are the most important person in your life.

This can seem like quite a peculiar thing to say!

People with children will often say: No my children are the most important thing in my life!

Wrong. Without you where would your children be?

You might think that a politician like Barack Obama, the President of the USA, is more important.

Wrong. For him to exist people like you must exist.

It is not Obama who makes the country run. It is people like you.

Also what is true is that people in positions like

Barack Obama have more opportunity to influence events at different levels than you.

However; in this context this does not mean that they are a more Important Person than you; they just have more opportunity.

You might say that your partner is more important than you.

Wrong. Without you who is there for that person to be "Part" of?

It is impossible to imagine all the little things and the big things that you have been a part of and which could only have happened with your participation or as the result of something that you did or contributed to.

No life is perfect. Anyone who tries to tell you that their life is, was and will be; is living a lie.

We all have Life Storms to contend with, rain that falls and bad weather of different types in our lives.

However; we learn about shelter, anticipating bad weather and about protecting ourselves and having about us that which we need for survival.

In all the lives that you touch and have touched; you also have to consider your own life.

- You may not value it much.

- You may feel like you are lost in the Shadows of life.

But the truth is that simply to be born into the world is an achievement of epic proportions.

To survive all the challenges of life and to get to the age that you are is an achievement of epic proportions.

To have awareness, consciousness, the ability to comprehend and the ability to physically move about the world means that you are an incredibly lucky person.

If all of this is not touching you then what about having some faith?

If you were not meant to be; would you be here?

If all things have a purpose; then mustn't you also have a purpose?

If you were meant to be here and you have a purpose; doesn't that make you a special person?

Regardless of how you may feel about yourself, what you need to understand is that there is an over-supply of certain things on this planet and no-one is going to be hurt by you taking your share.

What is there an abundance of?

- Self-Esteem is there in an inexhaustible supply for those who want it.

- As is Confidence.
- As is Feeling Good about yourself.
- As is Happiness.

You can take your fill of each of these as often as you like and you can never exhaust the supply.

If every person who has ever lived and who will ever live takes their fill of each of these they could never exhaust the supply.

You see each of us is given these when we are born and they exist within each of us for us to have and use.

It is only those who seek to control and influence others who may say that you have no right to:

- Be happy.
- Feel good about yourself.
- Be confident.
- Have terrific Self-Esteem

And here is another lesson.

We can seek to destroy these things and other peoples positive experiencing and enjoyment of them.

We may seek to punish and create discomfort for those who we see doing better than we are.

We may want to wreck the happiness and relationships of others because they have something which we envy and cannot have ourselves.

But what none of these Shadow dwellers can do is this:

> They cannot give you anything good or bad; all they can do is to create the conditions in which these things exist.

> It is through these conditions that they hope to reach your inner life and take control of you.

Often these Shadow dwellers try to convince us that they are the most important thing in our lives.

That they control the very air that we breathe and the very existence that we have.

In reality this is simply showing their true weakness.

They have the inability to live a good life without feeling that they have to hurt and control other people.

Destroying is an easy thing to do. Building positive, caring, forward looking lives is harder.

You see harming those who are less able than you is a sign of weakness and not strength. But some people achieve satisfaction from these types of behaviour.

Those who live in the Shadows often want us to adopt a value system that is based on corrupted values and standards that they want to control.

For the sake of having our own value systems that we are comfortable with; we will often look to others to supply them. And this is how we can be lead astray.

The reality is:

- Look into yourself first.
- What does that inner self of yours really want?
- Think of the people who you have really respected and admired through your life.

    Then consider what their view might be.

My own personal view of all of this is that we and the World are better when we try to do Positive things, in a Positive way, to achieve Positive outcomes that can be built upon and developed further.

If none of this has touched you then think of this:

If you are not prepared to value yourself and to take the opportunity to accept that you are the most important person in your life; then how can others do something that you are not prepared to do?

Accepting this simple premise of Self-Value does not mean that you will cease to be a human being.

- You will still have off days.

I personally call these my bear with a sore head days.

- You will still have the challenges of life to face and overcome.

And:

- You will have the opportunity to become the person you really want to be and that you really can become.

What a Fantastic Opportunity – Bring it on!

Allow ourselves the Temperance to accept that we are Imperfect People; and that we are all the better for it!

Notes: ....
....
....
....
....
....
....
....
....
....
....
....
....
....
....
....
....

Chapter 20

Begin the Journey!

The Chinese have a saying:

- Every journey begins with a single step.

I try to remember sayings like these for when times are difficult and just plain tough.

They help me to put things into perspective and to realise that if I keep going, I stand a chance of getting where I want to go. If I stop walking then I am not going any further.

Life is a journey for all of us. Every person on the planet has the same journey to undertake and their Confluence will be there with them.

Life really is what you try to make of it.

As human beings we are not going to get it right all the time. We need to allow ourselves the temperance to accept that we are Imperfect People.

As the Rivers of our Lives go along their paths we will experience and can learn from all of the things which happen to us: Both the good and the bad.

Sometimes it is not that which we survive which is the lesson and the experience of note. Instead it is the direction that it takes us in on its conclusion that is the lesson and experience which enriches our lives.

To understand how wonderful life can be we need to take the risk of living.

A common thing which I hear from people as they become older and begin looking back over their lives is:

> It is not the things which I have done which I regret so much as the things which I did not do; but wish that I had.

Now that you know that you are an Imperfect Person and you have permission to be Imperfect, make some mistakes and do some things wrong.

As an Imperfect Person you also have the opportunity to Improve your life, Live a Better life, Rise up to challenges and "Be" the person that you have the capacity to be.

This is the End of this book; and hopefully the beginning of something fantastic for you!

Notes: ....
....
....
....
....
....
....
....
....
....
....
....
....
....
....
....
....
....
....
....
....
....
....
....
....
....
....
....
....
....
....
....
....
....

About Guru David

Life would be great if it was perfect. Unfortunately life often falls short of perfection and often lacks clarity.

How do we make a better life in an imperfect world with lots of competing pressures?

Nature provides us with a lot of gifts that we can use to experience Life and to help us to be successful in whatever environment that we find ourselves in.

Unfortunately these gifts do not come with instructions and we need to learn through experience how to understand, interpret and manage these wonderful gifts.

Nature does not provide us with instruction manuals but it does provide us with special people who are able to help us with living our lives and making our living experiences the best that they can be.

Guru David is one of these special people.

Why would someone want to use a Guru?

Guru's tend to live a different life to normal people. They have different life experiences and they think and behave differently.

Guru's will often have encountered and overcome many types of hardships and difficulties. These will often be physical and cerebral and can occur over long periods of time, often decades.

Guru's will understand Humanity and Human Nature better and they often have insights and understanding of things that others do not.

Guru's make good guides, advisors and mentors when difficult, complex and challenging issues have to be addressed. They provide confidentiality and support as appropriate and help to achieve clarity of thoughts and actions.

A good Guru deals with reality and understands societies structures and pressures.

Meet an extra ordinary person

Guru David creates custom approaches for challenges that involve Feelings, Emotions, Psychology, Behaviours, Experiences, Knowledge and acquired Wisdom.

Guru David accepts selected personal and business clients that he feels that he can work with.

Guru David's approach includes using The Way of Vartis and his authoritative work with The Human Algorithm® Project.

A graduate of The College of The Richmond Fellowship; an experienced counsellor and therapist with specialist training, knowledge and experience of Alcohol and Drug Addiction with a high level of knowledge and experience working with dependency issues, problem architecture, problem dynamics and related Human Algorithm's®.

Guru David is an authority on working with Obesity and Weight Control issues and provides a customised approach that includes work from his books covering this subject.

Due to his work with problem architecture, problem dynamics and Human Algorithm's, Guru David is well placed to understand many different problem types and provide help to develop effective solution focused approaches.

Guru David's other books include understanding Motivation; working with Self Esteem and The Human Dynamics Matrix.

Guru David's other experiences and knowledge include obtaining black belts in martial arts, experienced in working with finance and debt resolution for members of the public, business consultancy, different levels of training, writing books and articles, being targeted by trolls, being victimised and abused for having a different view and behaviours, being targeted and the victim of financial crimes, experience around the music industry, innovation, design, building and an interest in different types of engineering, construction, physics and nature.

At different times, Guru David's resilience has inspired and amazed others and frustrated those who have tried to destroy him and his work.

Guru David has other knowledge, experiences and wisdom that can be revealed and shared at appropriate times.

Guru David would describe himself as spiritual rather than religious and this is evident in The Way of Vartis.

The Way of Vartis offers a view of the celestial reality of the universe, the truth about the future, the knowledge that people need to change how they live within their personal environments and the honesty of the reality of Life and why we are here.

The Way of Vartis provides an open approach and does not impose dogma. As a result someone can choose to add The Way of Vartis to their life and achieve the benefits without being required to give up any religious practices or beliefs they hold.

Guru David can be hired or consulted for specific or more general work.

Those who are interested in supporting The Way of Vartis or The Human Algorithm® Project can become a follower, supporter or sponsor.

Guru David can work in a variety of countries by arrangement and is comfortable to work through good quality interpreters.

Hello Readers!

You can find more information about the things that I am doing by visiting the following websites:

www.gurudavid.co.uk

www.vartis.co.uk

You can email me; Guru David with any comments or inquiries at: david@gurudavid.co.uk

The Vartis symbol

Intellectual Property Rights

Thank you for buying this book.

I hope that you found this book very useful and beneficial but please remember that this is not a license for anyone to use the material from this book.

If you want to use any of this material you will need to have permission to do so as years of work have gone into the creation and development of this material.

I am happy to hear from anyone who would like to have authorised use of this material and to discuss the terms of such use.

All Commercial use will be subject to licensing. Please see our website for contact information.

www.gurudavid.co.uk

Our Intellectual Property includes the following which is protected by Copyright, Trade Marks, Registered Trade Marks, Design Rights and Trade Secrets.

The Human Algorithm® Project

The Way of Vartis